Also by Elie Wiesel
with illustrations by Mark Podwal

The Golem

A Passover Haggadah

The Six Days of Destruction

King Solomon and His Magic Ring

The Tale of a Niggun

The Tale of a Niggun

ELIE WIESEL

ILLUSTRATIONS BY
Mark Podwal

INTRODUCTION BY
Elisha Wiesel

Schocken Books, New York

Text copyright © 1978 by Elirion Associates, Inc.
Illustrations copyright © 2020 by Mark Podwal
Introduction copyright © 2020 by Elisha Wiesel
Glossary copyright © 2020 by Schocken Books,
a division of Penguin Random House LLC, New York

The text of this work originally appeared, in slightly different form, as a
chapter in *Perspectives on Jews and Judaism: Essays in Honor of Wolfe Kelman*,
edited by Arthur A. Chiel (New York: Rabbinical Assembly, 1978).

Library of Congress Cataloging-in-Publication Data
Names: Wiesel, Elie, 1928–2016, author. Podwal, Mark H., [date]
illustrator. Wiesel, Elisha, [date] writer of introduction.
Title: The tale of a niggun / Elie Wiesel ; illustrations by Mark Podwal ;
introduction by Elisha Wiesel.
Description: First edition. New York : Schocken Books, 2020
Identifiers: LCCN 2020002648 (print). | LCCN 2020002649 (ebook).
ISBN 9780805243635 (hardcover). | ISBN 9780805243642 (ebook).
Subjects: LCSH: Holocaust, Jewish (1939–1945)—Poetry. LCGFT: Poetry.
Classification: LCC PQ2683.I32 T35 2020 (print) | LCC PQ2683.I32
(ebook) | DDC 841/.914—dc23
LC record available at lccn.loc.gov/2020002648
LC ebook record available at lccn.loc.gov/2020002649

www.schocken.com

Jacket illustration by Mark Podwal
Jacket design by Kelly Blair

Printed in China
First Edition

10 9 8 7 6 5 4 3 2 1

Introduction

Elisha Wiesel

"Why do you pray, Mr. Wiesel?"

I began to answer, but the questioner cut me off after just a sentence or two.

I realized he was right to do so. I had been giving him only a superficial reply, comparing the transcendent, otherworldly God of traditional Jewish belief with the false gods worshipped by our modern, materialistic society. It was a predictable response that invited challenge.

I needed to go deeper into the question.

And then I happened to find a tale to take me there.

The Tale of a Niggun, a narrative poem written by my father in the late 1970s, was a work of which I had been completely unaware. Set during World War II and on the eve of the Purim holiday, the poem tells the haunting, heartbreaking story of a rabbi who wrestled with a decision about the fate of a ghetto's Jews that no human being should ever have to confront. I did some research and discovered that my father had loosely based his story on actual, horrific events that had occurred during the war in European ghettos—most notably in two towns in central Poland, Zduńska Wola and Piotrków.

Some weeks later, I read the story aloud to the holy congregation of

New York's Carlebach Shul on the eve of Purim, as Ta'anit Esther drew to a close. As I described how my father's beloved, tortured rabbi communed with the sages from our past for guidance and solace, questions arose within me.

"Where is the IDF in this story, furious with a holy fire that they were not there to prevent the tragic outcome and swearing that this will never again happen to our people?" I could hear my cousin Steve asking.

"Where is Mordechai Anielewicz in this story, determined to take some of the enemy with him and show the world that Jewish blood is not cheap?" I could hear my friend Shmuley asking.

The answer to these questions is one that I would not have considered as a younger man. While there is something about the deaths of powerless Jews that seems to demand a coda filled with the heroics of the Israeli Army or the resistance fighters in the ghettos, my father's point was that this is not the only way for Jews to be heroes.

My father never carried a weapon, but he was a hero just the same. He fought with words, by telling his story and the stories of so many others, all of them heroes, too. He fought by infusing his stories with hope.

And that, to my surprise, gives me the answer to my challenger.

Why do I pray?

I pray because my father fought for memory, and so do I. He brought Jewish texts with him to Moscow for Simkhat Torah in the fall of 1965 and helped launch a movement to free our persecuted and imprisoned brothers and sisters by reporting what he saw and thought. He used his words to promote Jewish values, whether the victims were Jews or non-Jews.

Why do I pray?

Because I cannot separate my father from the Judaism he believed in, practiced, and wrote about. He was insistent that such a separation was impossible, even after what he saw and what he lived through. My father prayed every day, and I was blessed to see what living Judaism looked like in the way he treated people, the way he treated me, the way he treated knowledge, and the deep respect he paid to the past, present, and future. With him, as with the rabbi in this tale, the messenger became the message.

Why do I pray?

Because of the way my father's face lit up at the sounds of a niggun or a midrashic discussion. Because nobody sang or danced more fervently than he did on Simkhat Torah. Because we deserve the joy of connection across millennia that our ancestors felt. Because our children deserve to see us experiencing this joy.

And if you want to understand *how* my father prayed and not just why: Let us let go of words and join him, and the rabbi in this story, and Jewish people throughout the world in their synagogues this coming Friday night, as Shabbat begins and we are swept up into the niggunim being sung as daylight fades into holiness.

Publisher's Note

The text of *The Tale of a Niggun* was brought to our attention by Mechael Pomeranz, the proprietor of the iconic Jerusalem bookstore that bears his family name. One of Professor Wiesel's students for more than three decades, he is also the son of a survivor who is dedicated to ensuring that the Holocaust is remembered authentically. Mr. Pomeranz unearthed this treasure in an out-of-print collection of essays that had been published in 1978 in honor of the renowned Rabbi Wolfe Kelman, who had been a good friend of Professor Wiesel.

The Tale of a Niggun

A ghetto,
somewhere in the East,
during the reign of night,
under skies of copper
and fire.

The leaders of the community,
good people all,
courageous all,
fearing God and loving His Law,
came to see
the rabbi
who has cried and cried,
and has searched
darkness
for an answer
with such passion
that he no longer
can see.

It's urgent,
they tell him,
it's more than urgent;
it's a matter
of life or death

for some Jews
and perhaps
all Jews.

Speak,
says the rabbi,
tell me all:
I wish not to be spared.

This is what the enemy demands,
says the oldest
of the old Jews
to the rabbi,
who listens
breathlessly.
The enemy demands
ten Jews,
chosen by us
and handed over to him
before tomorrow evening.
Tomorrow is Purim,
and the enemy,
planning to avenge
Haman's ten sons,
will hang ten of our own,
says the oldest
of the old Jews.

mark podwal

And he asks:
What are we to do, rabbi?
Tell us what to do.

And his colleagues,
brave people
though frightened,
repeat after him:
What are we to do, rabbi?
Tell us what to do.

We are afraid,
says the oldest
of the old Jews,
afraid to make a decision—
afraid to make the wrong decision:
Help us, rabbi,
decide for us—and
in our place.

And the rabbi,
their guide,
feels his knees weakening,
the blood rushing to his face,
his chest is ready to burst,
and the room is turning,
turning,

turning around him,
and so is the earth,
and so are the skies,
and soon,
he feels,
he will fall
as falls the blind man,
a victim of night
and its prowlers.

He demands an answer,
says the oldest
of the old Jews,
the enemy demands an answer;
tell us what it must be,
our duty is to guide
just as ours is to follow.

What should we do
or say?
ask the leaders
of the ghetto
somewhere in the East
under forbidden
and cursed skies;
what can we do
so as not to be doomed?

. . .

But the rabbi is silent;
he dreams that he is dreaming,
that he has heard nothing,
lived nothing.
He dreams, the rabbi,
that he is someone else,
living somewhere else,
far away,
outside walls,
confronting other problems,
related to God
and not to death.

But the unhappy leaders
of the unhappy community
look at him,
and look at him
with such force,
such faith,
that he feels he must return
and speak.
Leave me,
he says with a weak but gentle voice,
I wish to be left alone.
I must think,
meditate,

I must go to the source,
explore the depth
and question
the past;
come back later,
I shall be waiting for you,
I promise,
yes,
I promise not to stay behind,
not to be spared.

Left to himself,
the rabbi,
breathing heavily,
rises from his chair
and goes to his bookshelves
to consult the Rambam,
who has foreseen
all situations
of all societies;
his decisions are clear
and precise,
simple and human,
humanly simple.
And the Rambam,
without hesitation,
recites for him

the immutable law
of tradition,
so harsh and so generous,
and so compassionate, too:
No community,
even when besieged,
may sacrifice
one of its members;
rather perish together
than hand over
to the enemy,
were he most implacable,
one of its children.

The rabbi of the ghetto understands
but refuses to accept:
The Law is beautiful,
he says,
the Law is luminous,
but
here we deal
not with ideas
nor with beauty
but with the destiny
of a community,
of a living community in Israel.

. . .

And the Rambam
answers with sadness:
I understand,
you *are* allowed to question
and even refute
my judgment,
though it is based
on justice
and law;
you *are* allowed to expect
another answer,
a more humane solution.
But,
brother in Israel,
brother in Torah,
understand me, too:
I have not foreseen,
I could not foresee,
your predicament,
your tragedy.
No, unfortunate rabbi,
no, poor brother of mine,
I,
Moshe son of Maimon,
can be of no help to you
or yours.

. . .

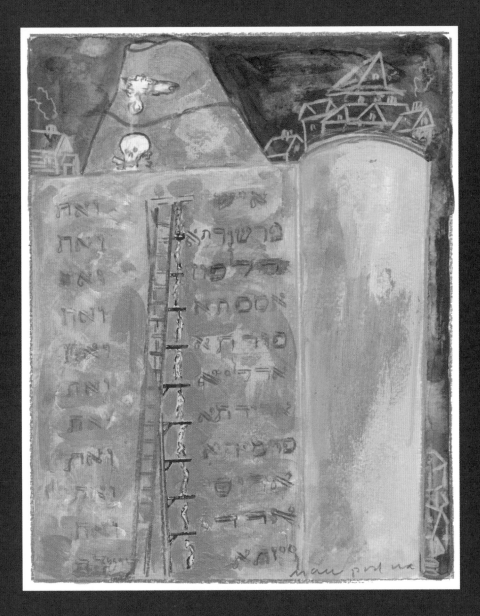

So, obstinate and tenacious,
the rabbi in the ghetto
turns toward other teachers,
some older
and some younger
than Rabeinu Moshe—
who knew much about Jewish suffering
but not enough about the cruelty
of the enemy.
He turns toward the
sages of Babylon
and Yavneh, the
legislators of Bnei Brak
and Fez, the
codifiers of France
and Spain,
and all, sadly,
shake their heads:
Rabbi, poor rabbi,
poor brother and colleague,
if he,
our teacher and guide,
Moshe ben Maimon,
if he cannot help you—
how could we?

. . .

And yet—
rejecting resignation,
the rabbi in the ghetto
goes from one to another,
asking again and again
his burning question:
You have taught me much
but not enough;
you have not told me
whether
I am to send ten Jews to the gallows
so as to save a thousand.
Whether
I am to condemn them all
and let them be massacred
so as to save Jewish honor,
so as to save
the Jewish soul,
which cannot die
and which dies nevertheless.
Where is truth, Rashi?
Where is justice, Rabbeinu Tam?
Which is the way,
Saadia Gaon,
which is the way
leading to Torah

and salvation
at the same time?

And all the sages,
all the commentators,
give him the same answer:
Forgive us,
young brother,
forgive us,
young colleague,
we cannot help you—
for our knowledge
cannot replace your own.

And so—
from book to book,
from century to century,
from guide to guide,
the rabbi comes to the Besht,
the most magnificent,
the most human,
the most brotherly
of sages and teachers.
And he breaks into sobs:
Israel, he says,
Israel son of Sarah,
you who consoled so many communities

in distress,
console us, too.
You who accomplished
so many miracles
for so many people,
intercede on our behalf.
I do not ask of you
to defeat the enemy,
nor even to revoke the decree;
all I ask of you
is to help me
find a solution.
If you know the solution,
share it with me,
for I do not know it:
all I know is
that there is night
around me
and in me;
and I am sinking,
drawn by its silence,
which is God's, too.

And the Besht,
faithful to his legend,
puts his arm around the rabbi's shoulder
and smiles at him,

and rather than talk,
begins to sing to him
a wondrous niggun,
a niggun without words,
a niggun that neither the Besht
nor anyone else
has ever sung before,
a niggun that
confers
hidden powers and privileges
that even angels and seraphim
do not possess;
he sings, the Besht,
and his face is shining,
for he is sure
that,
with this song,
he will be able
to break the chains
of evil
and malediction.

But
woe unto him
and woe unto us,
his niggun
is but a song of weakness,

a cry for help,
and not a weapon.

I know why this is so,
says the Besht
to the rabbi in the ghetto;
I know why
my powers have left me,
I know why:
my heart is heavy with pain,
too much pain,
and God dwells in joy—
in joy alone.
Help me,
young brother—
aren't you a rabbi in Israel,
the way I was?
Help me drive my sadness away,
and you will see,
you will see what can be
accomplished
with joy,
help me bring joy
into my heart!
But
the rabbi in the ghetto,

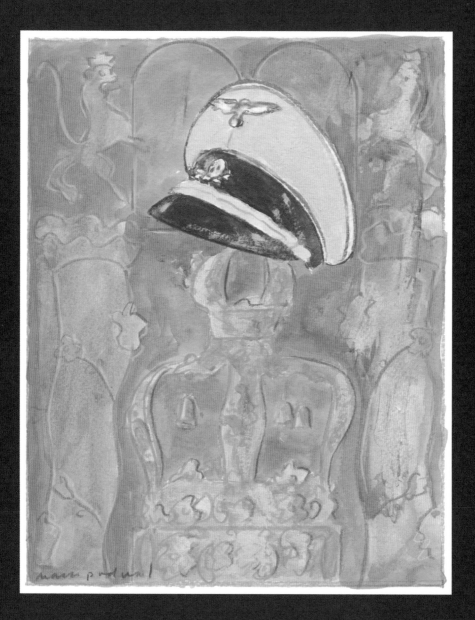

overcome by sadness,
is unable to help the Besht.

Well, says the Besht, then
I shall do it alone.
Let us start from the beginning.
I want to be joyous,
exuberant,
I want to sing in ecstasy
and dance,
and dance with all my being,
and shout my happiness
of being Jewish,
of being God's creature
participating in His work
and occupying His thought,
I want to open the gates of joy
and make it flood
the world below
and the world above,
and then
the murderer will be stopped
and the murder averted.

He tries, the Besht,
oh yes,
he tries hard,

he sings with all his strength,
he sings
and dances,
and calls for joy
to come
and take him
and free him
and us—
but
woe unto him
and woe unto us,
joy refuses to enter
his heart
and refuses to penetrate
his song.

Then the Besht,
his gaze extinguished,
admits his failure:
Forgive me
my young brother—
you are so near
and yet so far—
forgive me:
I am unable to help you—
someone does not want me
to help you.

. . .

Am I then to give up?
shouts the rabbi
in the ghetto.
No, says the Besht.
I must give up,
not you.
Be stronger than I am,
you are more needed
than I.

Nearing despair,
the rabbi knocks
at the gates
of the Besht's neighbor
and friendly rival:
Rabbi Eliyahu,
he says,
you help me!
My community has appointed me
its judge—
and I am helpless.

And so the Gaon Eliyahu
closes his books
and breaks his isolation,
and looks at the rabbi.

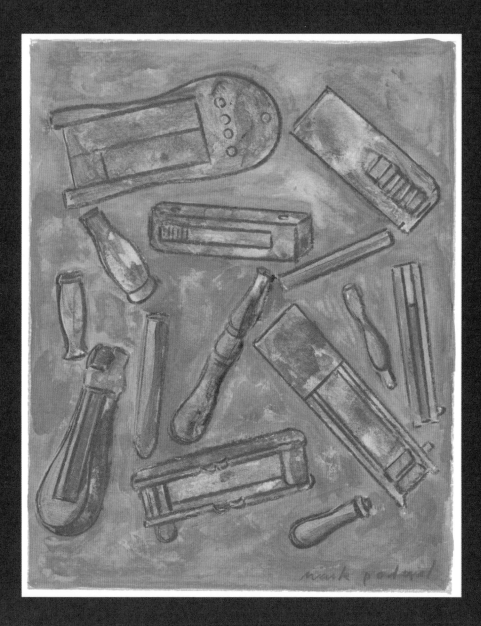

mark padnal

The light in his eyes
is the same
as that which enveloped Sinai
long ago:
Who are you? he asks.
I am a rabbi.
Where do you come from?
To what book do you belong?
I live in a ghetto,
says the rabbi.
I have a question
which no one is ready or able to answer—
perhaps this is a question
to which there is no answer.
Impossible, says the Gaon of Vilna.
All questions have answers!
Have you looked well?
Have you consulted
the proper sources?
Have you studied the Poskim
and their rulings?
Have you scrutinized the right texts?
And found nothing?
No sign,
no hint?
No?
Well—let us see,

let me think . . .
Ten names,
you said
the enemy demands
ten names,
right?
Yes, I see,
wait,
I see what is to be done,
wait—
here is the answer,
take it!
And the Gaon Eliyahu of Vilna
hands him
a piece of paper;
and the rabbi of the ghetto
takes it
and reads it,
incredulous,
and reads it again
and again:
one name,
always the same,
written ten times—
Eliyahu,
Eliyahu,
Eliyahu of Vilna,

ten times,
as is written
his own name, ten times . . .

Shattered and moved,
the rabbi whispers:
Thank you,
thank you
for showing me the way.

Now the rabbi is happy,
almost happy,
but suddenly
he hears someone calling him
with a caressing voice. It is Levi,
Levi Yitzhak of Berditchev.
I do not like that solution,
says the Berditchever Rebbe;
it pushes you into solitude
and this displeases me.
A Jew is never alone,
you ought to know that.
Even when he dies,
he does not die alone.
Self-sacrifice is not the answer,
my young brother
and peer.

When a Jew thinks he is lost,
he must find himself
within the community of Israel;
it must be strengthened
by him
and not divided;
if the enemy wishes to kill,
let him kill—
and do not tell him
whom to kill.
Your role,
my young brother and colleague,
the role of rabbi
is to be *with* his Jews,
not facing them.
Should they be summoned
by God
or the enemy,
should they choose
to respond,
do as they do,
walk with them,
pray with them
or *for* them,
howl with them,
weep as they weep;
share their anguish

and their anger
as you have shared their joy;
see to it
that the sacrifice
imposed by the enemy
unites his victims
instead of separating them;
as rabbi,
there is only one call
you must issue:
Jews stay together,
Jews
stay together
as Jews.

And so,
the next morning,
the rabbi receives
the eldest of the ghetto
and solemnly
informs them
of his decision:
the enemy will kill—
but his victims
will not be
our victims;
we shall remain

together
and together
we shall confront the enemy
as one person
linked by the same breath.

A few hours later
the word goes around
the sick streets
of the ghetto
somewhere
in the East
under hostile
and cruel skies.
And shortly before dusk,
at the hour when,
on the other side,
Jews everywhere gather
in their houses of study
and prayer,
to recite with gratitude
the miraculous events
surrounding Mordechai
and Esther
and their Jewish friends,
the enemy drives the inhabitants
of the ghetto

into the courtyard
of the old synagogue,
where the oldest of the old Jews
is ordered to make his decision known:
Who are the ten martyrs?
Who shall live, who shall die?

Taking one step forward,
showing no fear,
his entire being reflecting
dignity,
the oldest of the old Jews
declares firmly:
None of us
deserves
more than the other
either to live
or to die.
He waits a moment,
a long moment,
as though he wanted
to add
an explanation,
but changes his mind;
he takes one step backward
and is already
surrounded

by friends and allies.
Is the enemy disappointed?
Impossible to tell.
He moves his sleepy gaze
over the inhabitants
of the ghetto: young and old,
learned and not,
men and women,
children and their teachers,
all are here.
Is the enemy satisfied
that no one is missing?
Impossible to tell.
He looks at his victims
and says
simply,
coldly:
In one hour,
exactly one hour,
you will all be
dead.

And all the Jews,
in a single movement,
turn toward their rabbi
as though to ask for confirmation:
Is it true?

Elie Wiesel

Is it a dream perhaps?
A nightmare? A farce?
Some cry,
others smile,
 staring into emptiness.
Let us be ready,
says the rabbi.
He does not say
ready for what;
everybody knows.
Let us recite the *Vidui,*
all together,
says the rabbi,
and then
Sh'ma Yisrael,
all together;
let the Almighty hear our appeal,
perhaps He doesn't know
what is happening here below.
Therefore,
my friends,
my brothers,
we shall sing
loudly,
louder and louder,
do you hear me?
We shall sing so loud

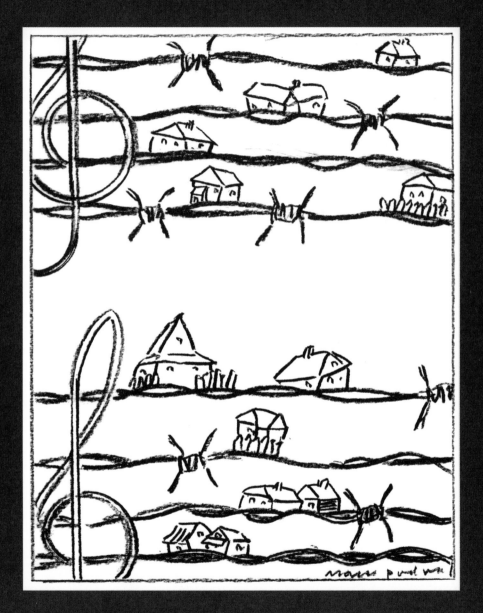

that our song will fill
heaven and earth ...
Some look at him
but do not understand;
others understand
but do not dare
to look at him;
there are those who wonder:
Sing?
You want us to sing,
rabbi?
Here? Now?
Yes! Now!
commands the rabbi.
I want you to sing now!
I am going to teach you
a song,
a niggun
that I have learned today—
a niggun meant
for this day!
And he begins to teach them
the niggun
that the Besht,
with his desperate fervor,
had sung for him
hours earlier.

. . .

And suddenly
the rabbi notices,
with joy mixed with anguish,
that the community,
his own,
is larger than he had thought.
From everywhere
Jews have come
to join it.
From Babylon
and Spain,
from Provence
and Morocco,
they have left the Talmud
to come here;
they have left the Tosafot
to come here;
they have left history
and legend
to be here,
present at this
upheaval of history;
they have left
their resting places
to come into this ghetto
to sing and dream

with these Jews
who are walking to their death.
Akiva and his disciples,
Bar Kochba and his warriors,
the sages
and the rebels,
the beggars and the princes,
the Holy Ari and his companions,
the Maggid and his disciples,
and the Gaon of Vilna,
strange,
he sings,
the Gaon of Vilna
sings the Besht's niggun,
as does the entire community,
as does the Besht himself,
while weeping
and dancing,
and celebrating
the Jew's loyalty
to his people
and to his song.

The enemy begins the massacre
but the niggun escapes him;
the slaughterer slaughters
but his victims,

one minute before their death,
aspire to immortality
and achieve it
with their song,
which does not,
cannot weaken,
cannot die:
it continues
and will continue,
until the end of time
and beyond.

Glossary

AKIVA (c. 50 CE–135 CE): One of the preeminent rabbinical scholars of the Mishnaic period (approximately the first two centuries of the Common Era) in the Land of Israel during its rule by the Roman Empire. He was executed by the Romans for refusing to stop teaching Torah to his students.

BAR KOCHBA (??–135 CE): Nom de guerre of Simon ben Kosevah, the military leader of the Judeans' final, ultimately unsuccessful revolt against the Roman Empire's rule; he kept the Roman Army at bay from his fortress in Betar for three and a half years. His nom de guerre, which means "son of a star," was given to him by Rabbi Akiva, who at one time believed him to be the Messiah.

BESHT (c. 1698–1760): Rabbi Israel ben Eliezer, also known as the Baal Shem Tov ("master of the good name") or Besht (its acronym). A mystic born in what was then southeastern Poland (now part of Ukraine), he was the founder of Hasidism, a sect of Judaism that emphasizes the spiritual, mystical, ecstatic, and populistic aspects of Jewish religious philosophy and practices.

BNEI BRAK: A city in ancient Israel, believed to be northeast of what is now Tel Aviv. Initially mentioned in the biblical Book of Joshua, it was known as a center of biblical scholarship in the Mishnaic period. Also a city in Israel today, founded in 1924.

ESTHER (fifth century BCE): The eponymous heroine of the biblical Book of Esther. The Jewish wife of Ahasuerus (believed to be Xerxes I), a fifth-century BCE king of the Persian Empire, she famously and dramatically saved the Jews of the empire from government-mandated genocide by revealing her Jewish origins to her husband in the presence of Haman, the king's vizier and anti-Semitic architect of the genocidal decree. Established the holiday of Purim with her cousin, Mordechai. See also HAMAN, MORDECHAI, and PURIM.

GAON OF VILNA; RABBI ELIYAHU (1720–1797): Rabbi Eliyahu ben Shlomo Zalman was the Lithuanian-born preeminent biblical scholar, Talmudic commentator, and decisor of Jewish law in eighteenth-century Europe. His scholarship influenced generations of rabbis who came after him.

HAMAN (fifth century BCE): The anti-Semitic vizier of the Persian king Ahasuerus and the villain in the Purim story, as narrated in the biblical Book of Esther. Haman was the driving force behind Ahasuerus's decree of genocide against the Jews of the Persian Empire; his plot was foiled by Esther, the king's Jewish wife, and he and his ten sons were hung on the gallows he had prepared for Mordechai. See also ESTHER, MORDECHAI, and PURIM.

HOLY ARI (1534–1572): Rabbi Isaac Luria Ashkenazi. Known as Ha'ari, he was born in Jerusalem, lived for a time in Egypt, and eventually settled in Safed, where he became a leading rabbi in Ottoman-era Palestine. He is considered to be the founder of contemporary kabbalah, the study of Jewish mysticism.

LEVI YITZHAK OF BERDITCHEV (1740–1809): One of the most beloved members of the second generation of Hasidic rabbis. A child prodigy from a dynasty of rabbis, he was a disciple of the Maggid of Mezritch (see entry below) and went on to become the rabbi of several communities in Poland, most famously Berditchev. Known for his compassion for all and advocacy before God for the Jewish people, he also composed popular religious folk songs that are sung to this day.

MAGGID (1700/1710?–1772): Also known as the Maggid of Mezritch. Rabbi Dov Ber Ben Avraham of Mezritch (a village in western Ukraine) was a leading disciple of the Baal Shem Tov (see entry above) and became his successor and the main architect of Hasidic Judaism. His circle of disciples spread Hasidism throughout Eastern Europe.

MORDECHAI (fifth century BCE): One of the main characters in the biblical Book of Esther. A leader of the Jewish community-in-exile in ancient Persia, he was also a member of King Ahasuerus's court. Cousin and guardian of the king's wife, Esther, he was instrumental in the king's nullification of his genocidal decree against the Jews of Persia. He and Esther established the Purim holiday to celebrate the triumph of the Jews over those who wished to destroy them. See also ESTHER, HAMAN, and PURIM.

NIGGUN (plural, NIGGUNIM): A type of religious song that can consist of biblical verses, classical Jewish poetry, and/or wordless melodic improvisation. It can be sung either as a lament or in joyous celebration. Niggunim are particularly employed in Hasidic prayer services and other religious celebrations.

POSKIM (singular, POSEK): Rabbis possessing unique scholarly and legal sensibilities who are regarded by their peers and communities as decisors of contemporary Jewish religious law. Their rulings are of particular importance where no obvious precedents exist in the Talmud and in medieval codes of Jewish law.

PURIM: A Jewish holiday that falls on the fourteenth day of the Hebrew month of Adar. It commemorates the victory, in the fifth century BCE, of the Jews of the Persian Empire over Haman, the anti-Semitic vizier of King Ahasuerus, who was the architect of a genocidal governmental decree against the Jews. The story of Purim, as recounted in the biblical Book of Esther, tells how the king's Jewish wife, Esther, and her cousin, Mordechai, were responsible for the nullification of the king's decree. Purim is celebrated by giving charity to the poor, exchanging gifts of food, a festive afternoon meal, and evening and morning readings of the Book of Esther. See also ESTHER, HAMAN, and MORDECHAI.

RABBEINU TAM (1100–1171): Rabbi Yaakov ben Meir, also known as Rabbeinu Tam, was a preeminent scholar, liturgical poet, Talmudic commentator, and decisor of Jewish law in the twelfth century. Born in France, he was a grandson of Rashi (see entry below) and considered one of the first Tosafists (see TOSAFOT below).

RAMBAM; RABEINU MOSHE (1138–1204): Rabbi Moshe ben Maimon, also known as Maimonides or by the acronym Rambam, was a towering figure in medieval Jewish philosophy, science, law, and Talmudic scholarship. Born in Spain, he fled persecution there and eventually settled in Egypt, where, in addition to writing groundbreaking works of Jewish law, philosophy, science, and scholarship, he served as head of the Jewish community, was a practicing physician, and was one of the court physicians to the sultan Saladin.

RASHI (1040–1105): Rabbi Shlomo Yitzchaki, also known by the acronym Rashi, was the French-born author of seminal and essential commentaries on the Bible and Talmud that have enabled centuries of beginning and advanced students to comprehend both the basic meaning of the text and more esoteric explanations. He also composed liturgical poems mourning the slaughter of German Jews during the First Crusade.

SAADIA GAON (882–942): Rabbi Saadia ben Yosef Al-Fayyumi wrote landmark works of biblical commentary, philosophy, Hebrew linguistics, and law. Born in Egypt, he studied under the rabbis of Tiberias and was eventually appointed the gaon, or head, of the legendary yeshiva in Sura, Babylonia (present-day Iraq). He wrote in Arabic as well as in Hebrew and is considered the founder of Judeo-Arabic literature.

SH'MA YISRAEL: The first two words of Deuteronomy 6:4, which capture the essence of Jewish belief. It is also the de facto name given to the compilation of several paragraph-long excerpts from the Bible that are recited as part of the morning, evening, and bedtime Jewish prayer services. The complete verse of Deuteronomy 6:4 is traditionally recited by Jews as they approach death.

SIMKHAT TORAH: A one-day holiday that occurs in the Hebrew month of Tishrei, following the Sukkot holiday. It celebrates the annual conclusion of the weekly Sabbath cycle of public readings from the Torah (with a reading from the last section of Deuteronomy) and the beginning of the new cycle (with a reading from the first section of Genesis). A festive occasion, it is also celebrated by carrying the Torah scrolls through the synagogue, in song and dance.

TA'ANIT ESTHER: The fast day that is observed on the day before Purim. It commemorates Queen Esther's decision to fast for three days before appearing, uninvited, before King Ahasuerus, setting in motion the chain of events that would result in the nullification of the decree of genocide against the Jews of the Persian Empire. See also ESTHER, HAMAN, MORDECHAI, and PURIM.

TOSAFOT: A compilation of several generations' worth of commentaries on the Talmud—in particular, on Rashi's commentary on the Talmud—by dozens of rabbis from France and Germany from the twelfth through the fourteenth centuries. The commentaries traditionally appear alongside the text of the Talmud on the outer side of each page, with Rashi's commentary appearing alongside the text of the Talmud on the inner side of the page. See also RASHI.

VIDUI: The Jewish deathbed confessional prayer that is also recited at several points during the Yom Kippur prayer service.

YAVNEH: A city in central Israel that traces its origins to the biblical era, as mentioned in the biblical book of 2 Chronicles. As Jerusalem was being besieged by the Roman Army in 67 CE, permission was given by the Roman commander Vespasian to Rabbi Yohanan ben Zakkai and his students to establish a yeshiva in Yavneh, which, with the destruction of the temple in Jerusalem in 70 CE, eventually became a center of Jewish life in the Land of Israel in the Roman and Byzantine eras and, for a time, the home of the Sanhedrin, the Jewish High Court. Conquered by an Islamic Army in the seventh century, it was re-established as a Jewish city in 1948.

A Note About the Author

The author of more than sixty works of fiction and nonfiction, Elie Wiesel was awarded the United States Congressional Gold Medal, the Presidential Medal of Freedom, the French Legion of Honor's Grand Cross, an honorary knighthood of the British Empire, and, in 1986, the Nobel Peace Prize. He was the Andrew W. Mellon Professor in the Humanities at Boston University for forty years, until his death in 2016.

A Note About the Illustrator

Mark Podwal has written and illustrated more than a dozen books, and has illustrated more than two dozen works by such authors as Elie Wiesel, Heinrich Heine, Harold Bloom, and Francine Prose. *King Solomon and His Magic Ring,* a collaboration with Wiesel, received the Silver Medal from the Society of Illustrators, and *You Never Know,* a collaboration with Prose, received a National Jewish Book Award. His art is represented in the collections of the Metropolitan Museum of Art, the Victoria and Albert Museum, Prague's National Gallery, and Jewish museums in Berlin, Vienna, Prague, and New York, among other venues. Honors he has received include being named Officer of the Order of Arts and Letters by the French government, the Jewish Cultural Achievement Award from the Foundation for Jewish Culture, and the Gratias Agit Prize from the Czech Ministry of Foreign Affairs.

A Note on the Type

This book was set in Albertina, the best known of the typefaces designed by Chris Brand (b. 1921 in Utrecht, The Netherlands). Issued by the Monotype Corporation in 1965, Albertina was one of the first text fonts made solely for photocomposition. It was first used to catalog the work of Stanley Morison and was exhibited in Brussels at the Albertina Library in 1966.

Composed by North Market Street Graphics,
Lancaster, Pennsylvania

Printed and bound by C&C Offset Printing Co. Ltd., China

Designed by Betty Lew